STUDY OF TEMPERAMENT

By

Gabriel Fur

TABLE OF CONTENTS

INTRODUCTION

Temperature is an important feature of social and emotional health. It describes the way we approach and react to the world; it is our personal style that is present from birth. If you have children or have spent time around children, you likely already have some understanding of temperament. Temperament is observable in infants from birth. Easy going children are generally happy, active children from birth who adjust easily to new situations and environments. Slow-to-warm children are generally observant, calm, and may need extra time to adjust to new situations. Children with active temperaments often have varied routine (e.g., eating, sleeping), and approach life with zest. Maybe the baby was often fussy and inconsolable. Some parents might even tell you that their child was so challenged, that they decided against having more children later. Other parents will happily report their child was an easy baby who handled new situations with great flexibility. In either example, the parents are thinking of their child's temperament. Furthermore, as an adult, the challenges faced with the physical/mental/psychological requirements to balance the expectations of certain deliverables and the reality of what is available to get that result is dependent on the temperament of that person whose result is expected.

CHAPTER 1

WHAT IS TEMPERAMENT

What are we trying to describe when we talk about Temperament? Is it something a person has inherited, something he has been trained and conditioned into, or something that he has caused to be developed by the exercising of his will? We use several terms to try and describe what we observe about individuals: Disposition, Inclination, Qualities, Traits, Nature, etc. It isobvious when we observe babies as well as adults that we see certain "God-given" talents, abilities, gifts, characteristics, temperaments, etc. Twins have been a most fascinating study in observing the differences between the two even though being born at the same time. Why these differences? Are they something we are all born with and will have until the day we die? Some advocate that we are given our basic temperament at birth and we will have it until we die.

Temperament refers to personal traits that determine how a person reacts to the world. It describes tendencies (styles in your behavior) that are just like patterns within the behavior of others. For instance, some people prefer to assume out loud while seeking to remedy the trouble. They anticipate that the answer will become obtrusive via discussion. Different human beings consider solutions in their very own minds, and when they talk, they voice their conclusions. If each type of human is operating on a project and they're blind to their specific approaches, they regularly experience conflict. For instance, Susan, who thinks out loud, turns annoyed while Jason criticizes her thoughts in advance. at the same time as she's simply trying to work out an answer, he assumes that her remarks represent a final thought for the solution. In evaluation, he needs time to get an answer in his head. Susan becomes annoyed because Jason isn't collaborating with her in working out a solution. Remember any other instance. One business enterprise's employees all get hold of the gift certificate on the end of the 12 months. They obtain their items with no notification or acknowledgment by using the administration. In every other company, no gift is given, but the president for my part goes round to each worker and offers particular examples of why he appreciates his or her work. One character may also experience fully preferred by way of receiving a gift certificate however wouldn't experience value through verbal acknowledgment; words without a few tangible gifts may additionally appear empty. For every other man or woman, the present certificates without any verbal appreciation may raise feelings of disappointment: "They're just attempting to shop for my loyalty."

The four temperatures described individuals as follows:

- **Sanguine (enthusiastic, energetic, and social)**

- **Choleric (short-tempered, speedy, and irritable)**

- **Melancholic (analytical, wise, and quiet)**

- **Phlegmatic (calm, self-controlled)**

CHAPTER 2

THE FOUR TEMPERAMENTS IN GENERAL

If we consider the reaction of various persons to the same experience, we will find that it is different in every one of them; it may be quick and lasting, or slow but lasting; or it may be quick but of short duration, or slow and of short duration. This manner of reaction, or the different degrees of excitability, is what we call "temperament." There are four temperaments: the choleric, the melancholic, the sanguine, and the phlegmatic.

The sanguine temperament is marked by quick but shallow, superficial excitability; the choleric by quick but strong and lasting; the melancholic temperament by slow but deep; the phlegmatic by slow but shallow excitability. The first two are also called extroverts, outgoing; the last two are introverts or reserved.

Temperament, then, is a fundamental disposition of the soul, which manifests itself whenever an impression is made upon the mind, be that impression caused by thought – by thinking about something or by representation through the imagination – or by external stimuli. Knowledge of the temperament of any person supplies the answer to the questions: How does this person deport himself? How does he feel moved to action whenever something impresses him strongly? For instance, how does he react, when he is praised or rebuked, when he is offended, when he feels sympathy for or aversion against somebody? Or, to use another example, how does he act if in a storm, or in a dark forest, or on a dark night the thought of imminent danger comes to him?

On such occasions one may ask the following questions:

1. Is the person under the influence of such impressions, thoughts, or facts, quickly and vehemently excited, or only slowly and superficially?

2. Does the person under such influences feel inclined to act at once, quickly, in order to oppose the impression; or does he feel more inclined to remain calm and to wait?

3. Does the excitement of the soul last for a long time or only for a moment? Does the impression continue, so that at the recollection of such impression the excitement is renewed? Or does he conquer such excitement speedily and easily, so that the remembrance of it does not produce a new

excitement?

The replies to these questions direct us to the four temperaments and furnish the key for the understanding of the temperament of each individual.

The choleric person is quickly and vehemently excited by any impression made; he tends to react immediately, and the impression lasts a long time and easily induces new excitement.

The person of sanguine temperament, like the choleric, is quickly and strongly excited by the slightest impression, and tends to react immediately, but the impression does not last; it soon fades away. The melancholic individual is at first only slightly excited by any impression received; a reaction does not set in at all or only after some time. But the impression remains deeply rooted, especially if new impressions of the same kind are repeated.

The phlegmatic person is only slightly excited by any impression made upon him; he has scarcely any inclination to react, and the impression vanishes quickly. The choleric and sanguine temperaments are active, the melancholic and phlegmatic temperaments are passive. The choleric and sanguine show a strong tendency to action; the melancholic and phlegmatic, on the contrary, are inclined to slow movement. The choleric and melancholic temperaments are of a passionate nature; they shake the very soul and act like an earthquake. The sanguine and phlegmatic are passionless temperaments; they do not lead to great and lasting mental excitement.

SANGUINE

Sanguine are optimistic, positive people in an apparently bad or difficult situation. They are cheerfully optimistic, sometimes to the point of seeming complacent, oblivious or naïve.

It is safe to say "A happy coronary heart makes the face joyful; however, heartache crushes the spirit."

An example of a disciple with such trait was Peter—(A Trust Me type). He was very dramatic, often talking up for the rest of the disciples. Occasionally he spoke before wondering. One moment, in front of the group, he promises to by no means forsake Christ. A while later he denied even understanding the Lord. He became possibly sanguine and choleric.

Sanguine human beings can be social, charismatic, and outgoing. They make pals easily. They are regularly the life of the celebration, or as a minimum, they're seen as first-class and advantageous, so they're normally appreciated by humans. However human beings with a sanguine temperament also can have trouble deeply investing themselves in their friendships. In other words, they may fall enticed by the amount of first-rate - popularity over real friendship. They can also be impulsive, shameless, self-absorbed, and forgetful. They can on occasion appear cold to individuals who need to have a deeper courting with them due to the fact they've trouble focusing their hearts on the connection. Human beings with a sanguine temperament also can battle with deep relationships because they are not continually precise at introspection. They can be very uncomfortable with silence and deep thought, and might sometimes also be uncomfortable with themselves.

Positive attributes of a sanguine

Full of energy: Sanguine people are usually the ones who never seem tired or down. They are quick-witted and people find them clever and funny.

Thrill seeking; They love adventure and new experiences.

Been social butterflies- They love been around people and they crave the energy of interacting with others.

Easy going; They usually don't take life seriously

and they are able to get over any conflict thar arise without much difficulty.

Optimistic- They have a positive outlook on life and can see the bright side of things.

Strong communicators; They love to talk and are able to convey information to others easily and comfortably, sharing ideas in a way that can interest others.

Confident: Generally, people with a sanguine temperament have a higher self-esteem and portray themselves as been confident in whom they are.

Mindful: Sanguine people often seem to live in the moment and don't focus too much on the past or present.

The sanguine person has many qualities on account

of which he fares well with his fellow men and endears himself to them.

a)   The sanguine is an extrovert; he readily makes acquaintance with other people, is very communicative, loquacious, and associates easily with strangers.

b)   He is friendly in speech and behavior and can pleasantly entertain his fellow men by his interesting narratives and witticisms.

c)   He is very pleasant and willing to oblige. He dispenses his acts of kindness not so coldly as a choleric, not so warmly and touchingly as the melancholic, but at least in such a jovial and pleasant way that they are graciously received.

d)   He is compassionate whenever a mishap befalls

his neighbor and is always ready to cheer him by a friendly remark.

e)   He has a remarkable faculty of drawing the attention of his fellow men to their faults without causing immediate and great displeasure. He does not find it hard to correct others. If it is necessary to inform someone of bad news, it is well to assign a person of sanguine temperament for this task.

f)   A sanguine is quickly excited by an offence and may show his anger violently and at times imprudently, but as soon as he has given vent to his wrath, he is again pleasant and bears no grudge.

1.   The sanguine person has many qualities by which he wins the affection of his superiors.

a)   He is pliable and docile. The virtue of

obedience, which is generally considered as difficult, is easy for him.

b)   He is candid and can easily make known to his superiors his difficulties, the state of his spiritual life, and even disgraceful sins.

c)   When punished he hardly ever shows resentment; he is not defiant and obstinate: It is easy for a superior to deal with sanguine subjects, but let him be on his guard! Sanguine subjects are prone to flatter the superior and show a servile attitude; thus quite unintentionally endangering the peace of a community. Choleric and especially melancholic persons do not reveal themselves so easily, because of their greater reserve, and should not be scolded or slighted or neglected by the superiors.

2.   The sanguine is not obdurate in evil: He is not stable in doing good things, neither is he consistent in doing evil. Nobody is so easily seduced, but on the other hand, nobody is so easily converted as the sanguine.

3.   The sanguine does not long over unpleasant happenings: Many things which cause a melancholic person a great deal of anxiety and trouble do not affect the sanguine in the least, because he is an optimist and as such overlooks difficulties and prefers to look at affairs from the sunny side. Even if the sanguine is occasionally exasperated and sad, he soon finds his balance again. His sadness does not last long, but gives way quickly to happiness. This sunny quality of the well trained sanguine person

helps him to find community life, for instance, in institutions, seminaries, convents much easier, and to overcome the difficulties of such life more readily than do choleric or melancholic persons. Sanguine persons can get along well even with persons generally difficult to work with.

Negative attributes of a Sanguine Temperament

Recklessness- Their tendency for thrill seeking can put them in unsafe situation that could harm themselves or others.

Impulsivity: They tend to make quick decision, might be irrational.

Poor concentration: They may bore easily and find it hard to stay focused on a task

Addictive personality; they often develop dependency on a substance that fed them through high need for excitement throughout their life.

Neediness: They often need reassurances of their positive attributes from others, even if they themselves feel confident. This can lead to a sense of neediness where the require a lot of reminders of their importance to others.

Attention seeking: They need so much reassurance from others that may struggle to feel completely devoted to their relationship; they never feel like one person can give them all the attention they need. This means that they end up engaging in activities that demands a lot of attention from crowds to show off their creativity and talents.

Mood swings: They can have mood swings and intense emotional outbursts without warning, which ends as soon as they start.

Self-complacency. The pride of the sanguine person does not manifest itself as inordinate ambition or obstinacy, as it does in the choleric, nor as fear of humiliation, as in the melancholic, but as a strong inclination to vanity and self-complacency. The sanguine person finds a well-nigh childish joy and satisfaction in his outward appearance, in his clothes and work. He loves to behold himself in the mirror. He feels happy when praised and is therefore very susceptible to flattery. By praise and flattery a sanguine person can easily be seduced to perform the most imprudent acts and even shameful sins.

Inclination to flirtation, jealousy and envy: The sanguine person is inclined to inordinate intimacy and flirtation, because he lacks deep spirituality and leans to the external and is willing to accept flatteries. However, his love is not deep and changes easily. An otherwise well-trained sanguine would be content with superficial familiarities as tokens of affection, but in consequence of his levity and readiness to yield, as well as on account of his optimistic belief that sin may have no evil consequences, he can be easily led to the most grievous aberrations. A bad woman with a sanguine temperament yields herself to sin without restraint and stifles the voice of conscience easily. Vanity and tendency to love-affairs lead the sanguine person to jealousy, envy, and to all the petty, mean, and detestable faults against charity, which are usually the consequence of envy. Because he is easily influenced by exterior impressions or feelings of sympathy or antipathy, it is hard for the sanguine person to be impartial and just. Superiors of this temperament often have favorites whom they prefer to others. The sanguine is greatly inclined to flatter those whom he loves.

Cheerfulness and inordinate love of pleasure: The sanguine person does not like to be alone; he loves company and amusement; he wants to enjoy life. In his amusements such a person can be very frivolous.

Other disadvantages of the sanguine temperament:

a)   The decisions of the sanguine person are likely to be wrong: Because his inquiry into things is only superficial and partial; also because he does not see difficulties; and finally because, through feelings of sympathy or antipathy he is inclined to partiality.

b)	The undertakings of the sanguine fail easily because he always takes success for granted: As a matter of course, and therefore do not give sufficient attention to possible obstacles, because he lacks perseverance, and his interest in things fades quickly.

c)	The sanguine is unstable in the pursuit of the good: He permits others to lead him and is therefore easily led astray, if he falls into the hands of unscrupulous persons. His enthusiasm is quickly aroused for the good, but it also vanishes quickly. With Peter he readily jumps out of the boat in order to walk on the water, but immediately he is afraid that he may drown. He hastily draws the sword with Peter to defend Jesus, but takes to flight a few minutes later. With Peter he defies the enemies of Jesus, only to deny Him in a short time.

d)   Self-knowledge of the sanguine person is deficient because he always caters to the external: And is loath to enter into himself, and to give deeper thought to his own actions.

e)   The life of prayer of the sanguine suffers from three obstacles: He finds great difficulty in the so called interior prayer for which a quiet, prolonged reflection is necessary; likewise in meditation, spiritual reading, and examination of conscience. He is easily distracted on account of his ever active senses and his uncontrolled imagination and is thereby prevented from attaining a deep and lasting recollection in God. At prayer a sanguine lays too much stress upon emotion and sensible consolation, and in consequence becomes easily disgusted during spiritual aridity.

METHOD OF SELF-TRAINING FOR THE SANGUINE

1.	A sanguine person must give himself to reflection on spiritual us well as temporal affairs. It is especially necessary for him to cultivate those exercises of prayer in which meditation prevails; for instance, morning meditation, spiritual reading, general and particular examination of conscience, meditation on the mysteries of the rosary, and the presence of God. Superficiality is the misfortune, reflection the salvation of the sanguine.

In regard to temporal affairs the sanguine person must continually bear in mind that he cannot do too much thinking about them: he must consider every point; anticipate all possible difficulties; he must not be overconfident, over optimistic.

2.   He must daily practice mortification of the senses, the eyes, ears, tongue, the sense of touch, and guard the palate against overindulging in exquisite foods and drinks.

3.   He must absolutely see to it that he be influenced by the good and not by the bad; that he accept counsel and direction. A practical aid against distraction is a strictly regulated life, and in a

community the faithful observance of the Rules.

4.   Prolonged spiritual aridity is a very salutary trial for him, because his unhealthy sentimentality is thereby cured or purified.

5.   He must cultivate his good traits, as charity, obedience, candor, cheerfulness, and sanctify these natural good qualities by supernatural motives. He must continually struggle against those faults to which he is so much inclined by his natural disposition, such as, vanity and self- complacency; love of particular friendships; sentimentality; sensuality; jealousy; levity; superficiality; instability.

DEALING WITH A SANGUINE PERSON

The education of the sanguine person is comparatively easy. He must be looked after; he must be told that he is not allowed to leave his work unfinished. His assertions, resolutions, and promises must not be taken too seriously; he must continually be checked as to whether he has really executed his work carefully. Flatteries must not be accepted from him and especially constant guard must be kept lest any preference be shown him on account of his affable disposition. It must be remembered that the sanguine person will not keep to himself what he is told or what he notices about anyone. It is advisable to think twice before taking a sanguine person into confidence.

In the education of a sanguine child the following points should be observed:

1.   The child must be consistently taught to

practice self-denial especially by subduing the senses. Perseverance at work and observance of order must be continually insisted upon.

2.   The child must be kept under strict supervision and guidance; he must be carefully guarded against bad company, because he can so easily be seduced.

3.   Leave to him his cheerfulness and let him have his fun, only guard him against overdoing it.

PHLEGMATIC

This is the easiest to get along with being congenial, happy, and people oriented. They make excellent administrators and other jobs that involve getting along with people. Phlegmatic has no fear of rejection and can handle unaffectionate and hostile people. Phlegmatic quite the opposite of the sanguine temperament, the phlegmatic temperament is commonly introspective and reflective. People with phlegmatic temperaments are cozy, quiet, and calm. They make few friends, but they're higher at forging strong, deep relationships. they also tend to be very devoted. Phlegmatic individuals tend to know other peoples deepest feelings and strive to build intimate attachments with just about everyone in their lives. They are interested in cooperation and interpersonal harmony, and this is why they preserve their family and friends. They could be described as considerate, charitable, sympathetic, trusting, warm, calm, relaxed, consistent, rational, curious and observant.

BRIGHT SIDE OF THE PHLEGMATIC

TEMPERAMENT

1. The phlegmatic works slowly, but perseveringly, if his work does not require much thinking.

2. He is not easily exasperated either by offenses, or by failures or sufferings. He remains composed, thoughtful, deliberate, and has a cold, sober, and practical judgment.

3. He has no intense passions and does not demand much of life.

DARK SIDE OF THE PHLEGMATIC TEMPERAMENT

1. He is very much inclined to ease, to eating and drinking; is lazy and neglects his duties.

2. He has no ambition, and does not aspire to lofty

things, not even in his piety.

THE TRAINING OF PHLEGMATIC CHILDREN

The training of phlegmatic children is very difficult, because external influence has little effect upon them and internal personal motives are lacking. It is necessary to explain everything most minutely to them, and repeat it again and again, so that at least some impression may be made to last, and to accustom them by patience and charity to follow strictly a well-planned rule of life. The application of corporal punishment is less dangerous in the education of phlegmatic children; it is much more beneficial to them than to other children, especially to those of choleric or melancholic temperament.

MELANCHOLY

Melancholy temperament has the proportion of depth of the concept of the phlegmatic temperament and the organizational prowess of the choleric temperament. They are introspective, deep thinkers. They love expertise and truth. They also can be creative, artistic, and awesome hassle solvers. However, humans with this temperament can also be prone to despair and moodiness. They may be perfectionists, waiting too much of themselves and in their buddies. They can be difficult to delight in. the more serious weak point of the melancholic temperament is its tendency to maintain onto hurts. Melancholic temperaments are slow to be moved to emotion, however, they're also gradual to transport out of their emotion. it could take a lot to get them

irritated, but they stay angry for a protracted, long

time. They are detailed and organized; the

melancholy is tempered by the outgoing and warm

sanguine. Melancholic are loyal, steadfast, stoic, and

pragmatic. Highly emotionally intelligent,

melancholic have an astute perspective about their

mental state and emotional state. They are strategic

people, reliable and dependable. In addition, they are

quick to ask for help, this stand, in stark juxtaposition

to their love of solitude, yet align with their nature

due to the need for space to decipher thoughts and

emotions.

Negative attributes of melancholy

When left emotionally unchecked, they demonstrate

nervousness, moodiness, or general anxiety.

Melancholic people have poor digestion, appetite, and circulation with predispositions to constipation and anorexia. They are prone to overthinking while also being quick to panic. However, if a person is able to manipulate these qualities, they can come closer to accomplishing goals, completing tasks and meeting deadlines.

BRIGHT SIDE OF THE MELANCHOLIC TEMPERAMENT

1.   The melancholic practices with ease and joy interior prayer. His serious view of life, his love of solitude, and his inclination to reflection are a great help to him in acquiring the interior life of prayer. He has, as it were, a natural inclination to piety.

Meditating on the perishable things of this world he thinks of the eternal; sojourning on earth he is attracted to Heaven. Many saints were of a melancholic temperament. This temperament causes difficulties at prayer, since the melancholic person easily loses courage in trials and sufferings and consequently lacks confidence in God, in his prayers, and can be very much distracted by pusillanimous and sad thoughts.

2.   In communication with God the melancholic finds a deep and indescribable peace. He, better than anyone else, understands the words of St. Augustine: "Thee, O Lord, have created us for yourself, and our heart finds no rest, until it rests in Thee." His heart, so capable of strong affections and lofty sentiments,

finds perfect peace in communion with God. This peace of heart he also feels in his sufferings, if he only preserves his confidence in God and his love for the Crucified.

3.   The melancholic is often a great benefactor to his fellow men. He guides others to God, is a good counselor in difficulties, and a prudent, trustworthy, and well-meaning superior. He has great sympathy with his fellow men and a keen desire to help them. If the confidence in God supports the melancholic and encourages him to action, he is willing to make great sacrifices for his neighbor and is strong and unshakable in the battle for ideals. Schubert, in his Psychology, says of the melancholic nature: "It has been the prevailing mental disposition of the most

sublime poets, artists, of the most profound thinkers,
the greatest inventors, legislators, and especially of
those spiritual giants who at their time made known
to their nations the entrance to a higher and blissful
world of the Divine, to which they themselves were
carried by an insatiable longing."

DARK SIDE OF THE MELANCHOLIC TEMPERAMENT

1.   The melancholic by committing sin falls into
the most terrible distress of mind, because in the
depth of his heart he is, more than those of other
temperaments, filled with a longing desire for God,
with a keen perception of the malice and
consequences of sin. The consciousness of being

separated from God by mortal sin has a crushing effect upon him. If he falls into grievous sin, it is hard for him to rise again, because confession, in which he is bound to humiliate himself deeply, is so hard for him. He is also in great danger of falling back into sin; because by his continual brooding over the sins committed he causes new temptations to arise. When tempted he indulges in sentimental moods, thus increasing the danger and the strength of temptations. To remain in a state of sin or even occasionally to relapse into sin may cause him a profound and lasting sadness, and rob him gradually of confidence in God and in himself. He says to himself: "I have not the strength to rise again and God does not help me either by His grace, for He does not love me but wants to damn me." This fatal condition can easily assume the proportion of despair.

2.   A melancholic person who has no confidence in God and love for the Cross falls into great despondency, inactivity, and even into despair. If he has confidence in God and love for the Crucified, he is led to God and sanctified more quickly by suffering mishaps, calumniation, unfair treatment, etc. But if these two virtues are lacking, his condition is very dangerous and pitiable. If sufferings, although little in themselves, befall him, the melancholic person, who has no confidence in God and love for Christ, becomes downcast and depressed, ill-humored and sensitive. He does not speak, or he speaks very little, is peevish and disconsolate and

keeps apart from his fellow men. Soon he loses courage to continue his work, and interest even in his professional occupation. He feels that he has nothing but sorrow and grief. Finally this disposition may culminate in actual despondency and despair.

3.   The melancholic who gives way to sad moods, falls into many faults against charity and becomes a real burden to his fellow men.

a)   He easily loses confidence in his fellow men, (especially Superiors, Confessors), because of slight defects which he discovers in them, or on account of corrections in small matters.

b)   He is vehemently exasperated and provoked by disorder or injustice. The cause of his exasperation is often justifiable, but rarely to the degree felt.

c)   He can hardly forgive offences. The first offense he ignores quite easily. But renewed offenses penetrate deeply into the soul and can hardly be forgotten. Strong aversion easily takes root in his heart against persons from whom he has suffered, or in whom he finds this or that fault. This aversion becomes so strong that he can hardly see these persons without new excitement, that he does not want to speak to them and is exasperated by the very thought of them. Usually this aversion is abandoned only after the melancholic is separated from persons who incurred his displeasure and at times only after months or even years.

d)   He is very suspicious. He rarely trusts people and is always afraid that others have a grudge against him. Thus he often and without cause entertains uncharitable and unjust suspicion about his neighbor, conjectures evil intentions, and fears dangers which do not exist at all.

e)   He sees everything from the dark side. He is peevish, always draws attention to the serious side of affairs, complains regularly about the perversion of people, bad times, downfall of morals, etc. His motto is: things grow worse all along. Offenses, mishaps, and obstacles he always considers much worse than they really are. The consequence is often excessive sadness, unfounded vexation about others, brooding for weeks and weeks on account of real or imaginary insults. Melancholic persons who give way to this disposition to look at everything through a dark glass, gradually become pessimists, that is, persons who always expect a bad result; hypochondriacs, that is, persons who complain continually of insignificant ailments and constantly fear grave sickness; misanthropes, that is, persons who suffer from fear and hatred of men.

f)   He finds peculiar difficulties in correcting people. As said above he is vehemently excited at the slightest disorder or injustice and feels obliged to correct such disorders, but at the same time he has very little skill or courage in making corrections. He deliberates long on how to express the correction; but when he is about to make it, the words fail him, or he goes about it so carefully, so tenderly and reluctantly that it can hardly be called a correction.

If the melancholic tries to master his timidity, he easily falls into the opposite fault of shouting his correction excitedly, angrily, in unsuited or scolding words, so that again his reproach loses its effect. This difficulty is the besetting cross of melancholic superiors. They are unable to discuss things with others; therefore, they swallow their grief and permit many disorders to creep in, although their conscience recognizes the duty to interfere. Melancholic educators, too, often commit the fault of keeping silent too long about a fault of their charges and when at last they are forced to speak, they do it in such an unfortunate and harsh manner, that the pupils become discouraged and frightened by such admonitions, instead of being encouraged and directed.

METHOD OF SELF-TRAINING FOR THE MELANCHOLIC PERSON

1.   The melancholic must cultivate great confidence in God and love for suffering, for his spiritual and temporal welfare depend on these two virtues. Confidence in God and love of the Crucified are the two pillars on which he will rest so firmly, that he will not succumb to the most severe trials arising from his temperament. The misfortune of the melancholic consists in refusing to carry his cross; his salvation will be found in the voluntary and joyful bearing of that cross.

2.   He should always, especially during attacks of melancholy, say to himself:" It is not so bad as I

imagine. I see things too darkly," or "I am a pessimist."

3.   He must from the very beginning resist every feeling of aversion, diffidence, discouragement, or despondency, so that these evil impressions can take no root in the soul.

4.   He must keep himself continually occupied, so that he finds no time for brooding. Persevering work will master all.

5.   He is bound to cultivate the good side of his temperament and especially his inclination to interior life and his sympathy for suffering fellow men. He must struggle continually against his weaknesses.

IMPORTANT POINTS IN THE TRAINING OF THE MELANCHOLIC

In the treatment of the melancholic special attention must be given to the following points:

1.   It is necessary to have a sympathetic understanding of the melancholic. In his entire deportment he presents many riddles to those who do not understand the peculiarities of the melancholic temperament. It is necessary, therefore, to study it and at the same time to find out how this temperament manifests itself in each individual. Without this knowledge great mistakes cannot be avoided.

2.   It is necessary to gain the confidence of the melancholic person. This is not at all easy and can be done only by giving him a good example in everything and by manifesting an unselfish and

sincere love for him. Like an unfolding bud opens to the sun, so the heart of the melancholic person opens to the sunshine of kindness and love.

3. One must always encourage him. Friendly advice and patience with his slow actions give him courage and vigor. He will show himself very grateful for such kindness.

4. It is well to keep him always busy, but do not overburden him with work.

5. Because melancholics take everything to heart and are very sensitive, they are in great danger of weakening their nerves. It is necessary, therefore, to watch nervous troubles of those entrusted to one's care. Melancholics who suffer a nervous breakdown are in a very bad state and cannot recover very easily.

6.   In the training of a melancholic child, special care must be taken to be always kind and friendly, to encourage and keep him busy. The child, moreover, must be taught always to pronounce words properly, to use his five senses, and to cultivate piety. Special care must be observed in the punishment of the melancholic child, otherwise obstinacy and excessive reserve may result. Necessary punishment must be given with precaution and great kindness and the slightest appearance of injustice must be carefully avoided.

FUNDAMENTAL DISPOSITION OF THE MELANCHOLIC

1.   Inclination to reflection. The thinking of the

melancholic easily turns into reflection. The thoughts of the melancholic are far reaching. He dwells with pleasure upon the past and is preoccupied by occurrences of the long ago; he is penetrating; is not satisfied with the superficial, searches for the cause and correlation of things; seeks the laws which affect human life, the principles according to which man should act. His thoughts are of a wide range; he looks ahead into the future; ascends to the eternal. The melancholic is of an extremely soft-hearted disposition. His very thoughts arouse his own sympathy and are accompanied by a mysterious longing. Often they stir him up profoundly, particularly religious reflections or plans which he cherishes; yet he hardly permits his fierce excitement to be noticed outwardly. The untrained melancholic is easily given to brooding and to day-dreaming.

2.   Love of retirement. The melancholic does not

feel at home among a crowd for any length of time;

he loves silence and solitude. Being inclined to

introspection he secludes himself from the crowds,

forgets his environment, and makes poor use of his

senses – eyes, ears, etc. In company he is often

distracted, because he is absorbed by his own

thoughts. By reason of his lack of observation and his

dreaming the melancholic person has many a mishap

in his daily life and at his work.

3.   Serious conception of life. The melancholic

looks at life always from the serious side. At the core

of his heart there is always a certain sadness, 'a

weeping of the heart,' not because the melancholic is

sick or morbid, as many claim, but because he is permeated with a strong longing for an ultimate good (God) and eternity, and feels continually hampered by earthly and temporal affairs and impeded in his cravings. The melancholic is a stranger here below and feels homesick for God and eternity.

4.   Inclination to passivity. The melancholic is a passive temperament. The person possessing such a temperament, therefore, has not the vivacious, quick, progressive, active propensity, of the choleric or sanguine, but is slow, pensive, reflective. It is difficult to move him to quick action, since he has a marked inclination to passivity and inactivity. This pensive propensity of the melancholic accounts for his fear of suffering and difficulties as well as for his

dread of interior exertion and self-denial.

CHOLERIC

The choleric is the most active of the four temperaments. Choleric personalities are hot, dry, fiery, creatures. At their best they are ambitious, brave and proud, but they can also be violent, deceitful and violent. And without exception, they are irritable and bad-tempered. The choleric is attracted to the peaceful, calm and good-natured phlegmatic, while the phlegmatic is drawn to the choleric energy and takes charge temperament, the one who comes up with all the activities and moves and the relationship along. The choleric temperament is the rarest of the four primary types. Those with a choleric temperament are results-driven by making goals and sticking with them until they are complete. Thus, they exhibit a positive demeanor or disposition and are constantly moving forward. Choleric on, like melancholic are more attuned to ideals than relationships. Avoid the talk of hurt feelings and delve into justice, honor, and appropriate behavior. Choleric children like all children take patience. They blow up, fall apart, scream, be physical- and the best thing you can do is be calm.

CHARACTERISTICS OF THE CHOLERIC TEMPERAMENT

A choleric person shows his energy so much the more and perseveres also under great difficulties until he has reached his goal. Pusillanimity or despondency the choleric does not know. The

choleric person is quickly and vehemently excited by

any and every influence. Immediately the reaction

sets in and the impression remains a long time. The

choleric man is a man of enthusiasm; he is not

satisfied with the ordinary, but aspires after great and

lofty things. He craves for great success in temporal

affairs; he seeks large fortunes, a vast business, an

elegant home, a distinguished reputation or a

predominant position. He aspires to the highest also

in matters spiritual; he is swayed with a consuming

fire for holiness; he is filled with a yearning desire to

make great sacrifices for God and his neighbor, to

lead many souls to heaven.

The natural virtue of the choleric is ambition; his

desire to excel and succeed despises the little and vulgar, and aspires to the noble and heroic. In his aspiration for great things the choleric is supported by:

1.   A keen intellect. The choleric person is not always, but usually endowed with considerable intelligence. He is a man of reason while his imagination and his emotions are poor and stunted. It is said that Julius Caesar was able to dictate different letters to several secretaries at the same time without losing the line of thought for each dictation.

2.   A strong will. He is not frightened by difficulties, but in case of obstacles

3.   Strong passions. The choleric is very passionate. Whenever the choleric is bent upon

carrying out his plans or finds opposition, he is filled with passionate excitement. All dictators, old and new, are proof of this statement.

4.   An often times subconscious impulse to dominate others and make them subservient. The choleric is made to rule. He feels happy when he is in a position to command, to draw others to him, and to organize large groups.

A very great impediment for the choleric in his yearning for great things is his imprudent haste. The choleric is immediately and totally absorbed by the aim he has in mind and rushes for his goal with great haste and impetuosity; he considers but too little whether he can really reach his goal.

DARK SIDES OF THE CHOLERIC TEMPERAMENT

Pride which shows itself in the following instances:

a)   The choleric is full of himself. He has a great opinion of his good qualities and his successful work and considers himself as something extraordinary and as one called upon to perform great feats. He considers even his very defects as being justified, nay, as something great and worthy of praise; for instance, his pride, his obstinacy, his anger.

b)   The choleric is very stubborn and opinionated. He thinks he is always right, wants to have the last word, tolerates no contradiction, and is never willing to give in.

c)   The choleric has a great deal of self-confidence. He relies too much upon his own knowledge and ability. He refuses the help of others and prefers to work alone, partly because he does not like to ask for help, partly because he believes that he is himself more capable than others and is sure to succeed without the help of others.

d)   The choleric despises his fellow man. To his mind others are ignorant, weak, unskilled, and slow, at least when compared with himself. He shows his contempt of his neighbor by despising, mocking, making belittling remarks about others and by his proud behavior toward those around him, especially toward his subjects.

e)   The choleric is domineering and inordinately ambitious. He wants to hold the first place, to be admired by others, to subject others to himself. He belittles, combats, even persecutes by unfair means those who dare to oppose his ambition.

f)	The choleric feels deeply hurt when he is humiliated or put to shame. Even the recollection of his sins fills him with great displeasure because these sins give him a lower opinion of himself. In his disgust over his sins he may even defy God Himself.

2.	Anger. The choleric is vehemently excited by contradiction, resistance, and personal offenses. This excitement manifests itself in harsh words which may seem very decent and polite as far as phrasing is concerned, but hurt to the core by the tone in which they are spoken. Nobody can hurt his fellow man with a few words more bitterly than a choleric person. Things are made even worse by the fact that the choleric in his angry impetuosity makes false and exaggerated reproaches, and may go so far in his passion, as to misconstrue the intentions and to pervert the words of those who irritated him, thus, blaming with the sharpest of expressions, faults which in reality were not committed at all. By such injustice, which the choleric inflicts in his anger upon his neighbor he can offend and alienate even his best friends.

The choleric may even indulge in furious outbursts of anger. His anger easily degenerates into hatred. Grievous offenses he cannot forget. In his anger and pride he permits himself to be drawn to actions which he knows will be very detrimental to himself and to others; for instance, ruin of his health, his work, his fortune, loss of his position, and complete rupture with intimate friends. By reason of his pride and anger he may totally ignore and cast aside the very plans for the realization of which he has worked for years.

3.   Deceit, disguise and hypocrisy. As noble and magnanimous as the choleric is by nature, the tendency to pride and self-will may lead him to the lowest of vices, deceit and hypocrisy. He practices deceit, because he is in no way willing to concede that he succumbed to a weakness and suffered a defeat. He uses hypocrisy, deception, and even outright lies, if he realizes that he cannot carry out his plans by force.

For the true Communist everything that will help his

cause is right and just: he makes and breaks treaties and promises; robbery and lies and murder are considered justified if done for the Party and the Cause, without consideration of the cost in human suffering.

4.   Lack of sympathy. The choleric, as said above, is a man of reason. He has two heads but no heart. This lack of human sentiment and sympathy is, in a way, of great advantage to him. He does not find it hard to be deprived of sensible consolations in prayer and to remain a long time in spiritual aridity. Effeminate, sentimental dispositions are repugnant to him; he hates the caresses and sentimentality which arise between intimate friends. False sympathy cannot influence him to neglect his duties or abandon

his principles. On the other hand, this lack of sympathy has its great disadvantages. The choleric can be extremely hard, heartless, even cruel in regard to the sufferings of others. He can cold-bloodedly trample upon the welfare of others, if he cannot otherwise reach his goal. Choleric superiors should examine their conscience daily, to discover whether they have not shown a lack of sympathy toward their subjects, especially if these are sickly, less talented, fatigued, or elderly.

Most people have a mixed temperament. Some persons, however, have one predominant temperament, for instance, the choleric; but the fundamental characteristics, the light and dark sides of this principal temperament are extenuated or accentuated by the influence of the other temperaments. In general, a person is happier if his temperament is not a pure one. The combination shapes the rough edges of the main temperament. In order to facilitate the recognition of one's own temperament these mixtures of temperaments are herewith mentioned briefly.

1.   In the choleric-sanguine temperament the excitement is quick, and the reaction also; but the impression is not so lasting as with the pure choleric temperament.

The pride of the choleric is mixed with vanity; the anger and obstinacy are not so strong, but more moderate than in the pure choleric. This is a very happy combination.

2.	The sanguine-choleric temperament is similar to the choleric-sanguine temperament; only the sanguine characteristics prevail, the choleric ones recede to the background. Excitement and reaction are quick and vehement and the impression does not fade so quickly as with the pure sanguine, even though it does not penetrate so far as with the pure choleric. The sanguine fickleness, superficiality, extroversion, and garrulity are mitigated by the seriousness and stability of the choleric.

3.	The choleric-melancholic and the melancholic-choleric temperaments. In this one, two serious, passionate temperaments are mixed; the pride, obstinacy, and anger of the choleric with the morose, unsocial, reserved temper of the melancholic.

Persons who have such a mixture of temperaments must cultivate a great deal of self-control, in order to acquire interior peace and not to become a burden to those with whom they work and live.

4.   The melancholic-sanguine temperament. In this the impressions are feeble, the reaction is weak, and it does not last as long as with the pure melancholic. The sanguine gives to the melancholic something flexible, friendly, and cheerful. The melancholic persons with a sanguine alloy are those cordial, soft-hearted people who cannot bear to hurt anyone, are quickly touched, hut unfortunately also fail where energy and strength are needed. Sanguine persons with a melancholic mixture are similar. Only in this

case the sanguine superficiality and inconstancy prevail.

5.The melancholic-phlegmatic temperament. People of this type succeed better in community life than the pure melancholic. They lack, more or less, the morose, gloomy, brooding propensity of the melancholic and are happily aided by the quiet apathy of the phlegmatic. Such people do not easily take offense.

Study of Temperament

CHAPTER 3

TEMPERAMENTS AND CHRISTAINITY

This concept has survived via the centuries in its ancient form, but, it is usually as a psychological truth instead of a biological one. The reactions of the sanguine individual are quick and quick-lived. He is effortlessly aroused and brief to forget about. He enjoys reports and the agency of others and is a favorite at parties for his heat and vivacious personality. He may have many friends, at least on the surface level, and be inquisitive about many stuff, however, might not have the attention span to master them. certainly one of his best strengths within the spiritual life is that he finds obedience easier than a number of the alternative temperament kinds, being affable and willing to 'cross along' with others. This,

of direction, can also be his downfall and matched

with impulsivity, ought to make him susceptible to

sins towards chastity and temperance. He will work

difficult to grasp himself however if he does, can be a

notable contributor to the kingdom, evangelizing his

many pals and drawing them into the greatest journey

to be had. The choleric is decisive. Consequently, his

reactions may be short and long-lasting. This is the

crucial leader temperament: aggressive, assured, and

direct. The choleric will tend to be aim-orientated.

He'll see the large photograph however possibly no

longer the people he may need to assist him to

accomplish it if he'll let them for he tends to love to

do things himself. in the end, he figures, he can do it

great. Now not sudden, this man or woman will battle

with pleasure extra than the others.

Relationships can be difficult with him; an inclination to insensitivity can be a task to genuine intimacy and vulnerability. However the Spirit-led choleric will enthusiastically have the imaginative and prescient stamina to determine and reform orders and institutions and lead holy armies of saints inside the spiritual battlefield. The melancholic person is not inspired fast, but as soon as she is, will "no longer neglect without difficulty," Melancholic are prone to solitude, mirrored images, and introspection. They can be bad and skeptical, and discover it difficult to 'appearance on the bright aspect.' This may paralyze them in the face of a difficult project: wherein the sanguine doesn't assume in advance, and the choleric is prepared to address difficulties head-on, the melancholic tends to procrastinate as she mulls pessimistically over the whole thing that would cross wrong. They had exceptional attention to element however within the religious realm, this will make scrupulosity an actual chance. However, the melancholic could have the easiest time of the four temperaments establishing a prayer lifestyle. Intimacy with God will come very evidently to one so reflective and thoughtful, and melancholic may additionally make the greatest mystics. Ultimately, the phlegmatic. A phlegmatic is aroused with a problem and handiest weakly. When he's, it is of brief duration. They tend to be affected person, orderly, measured, and without robust feelings. They are peaceful and sluggish-shifting, unswerving, and committed. But these tranquil people frequently have an iron that will hide below their calm outdoors. Introverted like the melancholic, leadership might not come evidently to them and they may choose to comply with, and they may be the most dependable and committed of fans. The phlegmatic might probably accept Church coaching without question, for instance, but might also want more encouragement to take an active position in evangelism and challenge.

CHAPTER 4

TEMPERAMENTS AND HUMAN PSYCHOLOGY

In psychology, temperament widely refers to regular man or woman differences in behavior which are biologically primarily based and are relatively unbiased of studying, machine of values and attitudes. temperament, in psychology, an aspect of personality concerned with emotional dispositions and reactions and their speed and intensity; the term often is used to refer to the prevailing mood or mood pattern of a person.

There are nine specific developments of temperament:

1.   Interest level

2.   Biological rhythms

3.   Sensitivity

4.   Intensity of response

5.   Adaptability

6.   technique/withdrawal

7.   Staying power

8.   Distractibility

9.   Temper

Every individual has their very own unique mixture of character or temperament traits, so you will be much like any other character or your baby on one trait and one-of-a-kind on another. These developments are a part of a person's personality and one of the ways that make every one of us particular.

There's no right or incorrect temperament—all and sundry have their specific style of wondering, acting, and interacting with the arena.

PARENTING AND TEMPERAMENT

Temperament can describe or convey context to your child's behavior. For instance, if your baby is a picky eater, that can be very frustrating. But, if you apprehend your infant is very sensitive to texture and touch, which could assist explain their conduct that can alternate the way you feel about it and the way you react to it. Understanding your toddler's temperament can even help you have got suitable expectations for them. Just like its no longer honest to count on a little one to wait patiently, it's no longer honest to assume a baby who's "sluggish to heat up" or tends to withdraw to jump into a new play institution or play with different youngsters on the playground proper away. Now and again your temperament is very much like your child's, and from time to time or in some specific approaches it could be very extraordinary. When patterns are similar, it is probably very smooth to parent your child, but when they're specific or in the unique approaches or conditions whilst they are exclusive, it can be very challenging. Taking the time to apprehend your baby's temperament and the ways it is similar or exclusive to your very own allow you to adapt your parenting to build for your infant's strengths and meet their precise desires. While you don't apprehend your toddler's behavior or you're suffering with an ordinary like bedtime, diapering, or grocery buying, take a minute to consider whether or not that warfare is associated with your child's temperament. If it is, you will be able to make small modifications to your expectations, routines, or strategies which could make matters simpler for you and your baby.

Interest Levels

Interest stage refers to how bodily energetic someone is. A few people experience the need to be up and shifting and on the cross all of the time, whereas different people are much more likely to transport extra slowly and interact in quieter, calmer sports.

High-Interest degree

High-interest degree kids who have got a high-interest stage can also switch quickly from one hobby to any other. You may think of their conduct as rowdy and might see them as disruptive or boisterous. in the course of sluggish or quiet sports, high lively kids may additionally have trouble sitting nonetheless and will in all likelihood be fidgety.

Biological Rhythms

Organic rhythms: information on your child's organic measure allows you to recognize and help your baby. Everyday rhythms: are kids, who have normal rhythms, they will effortlessly stick to a habit. It is going to be smooth for them to eat meals and snacks at the same time each day, nap and sleep, and even bathroom at the same time each day. This makes it smooth for mother and father to have a predictable recurring.

Abnormal rhythms

Children with abnormal rhythms will have varying schedules because their styles are irregular. It will be hard for them to nap, consume, or lavatory at an equal time every day. it may be difficult for these youngsters to paste to a strict every day habitual, as they may no longer experience tiredness at the same time every day. When you understand your infant's organic rhythms, it could be less difficult to install your expectations or your day-by-day agenda in your baby to achieve success and to avoid pressure for you and your infant. in case your child is rather every day, you may set each day time table and do your high-quality to stick to it. in case your baby has rhythms that might be extra irregular, it could be useful to have an extra flexible routine when feasible.

Sensitivity

Knowledge of your baby's sensitivity permits you to understand and aid your child.

High sensitivity: exceptionally sensitive children may react very strongly to their surroundings. They may be disenchanted by way of the sounds of a loud truck out of doors or using vibrant fluorescent lighting. They react to the slightest stimuli which can appear harmless to every person else or even go neglected.

Low sensitivity: children with low sensitivity won't be bothered by subtle stimuli, like sounds or textures. Their reactions won't be as strong whilst they are impacted via something; they'll now not cry after they cave in, even though they may be harmed. Considering your toddler's sensitivity permits you to have greater fantastic interactions with them. if your especially touchy baby is concerned about uncomfortable clothes, take them to the store to help you choose out garments that might be comfortable for them. You could additionally want to give them extra time inside the morning to dress to ensure they find a secure outfit. Similarly, they will need time and a quiet area while you are at a circle of relatives gathering or a celebration. You could additionally want to be extra tuned in in your low sensitivity baby, as they may no longer react strongly whilst they are hurt, ill, or troubled through something. By way of tuning in and paying attention, you could ensure you're privy to and assembly their desires.

Letting your everyday agenda and expectancies vary

to fulfill your infant's sensitivity can prevent struggle

and strain, and permit your toddler to have their

needs met in a manner that plays to their strengths

and builds upon their natural temperament.

The intensity of reaction

Excessive depth: extra excessive children can have

very effective reactions to things. When something

terrible occurs, their reaction can be very robust even

though the scenario isn't serious. For instance, if they

need to wear their favored pink shirt and it's in the

washing machine, they will have a severe outburst.

Similarly, they will be difficult to contain even when

effective things occur. Youngsters with excessive

intensity reactions may be classified as dramatic and it can appear to be they're making a huge deal out of not anything.

Low intensity:

Youngsters with low intensity will react very mildly to negative and fine situations. They will have a limited reaction to things that manifest to them or might not seem to react a lot at all. It may be hard to understand how a low-intensity baby is feeling. Understand that your infant's sturdy reactions are part of their temperament and assist them to analyze appropriate methods to specify the robust emotional reactions. For low-intensity children, it's miles regularly harder for parents to apprehend how their low-intensity toddler is feeling due to the fact they may now not show the one feelings of their reactions or will no longer show them very strongly. Understanding that your child is low intensity, you can paint on choosing up on your toddler's cues and even asking about their emotions so that you are tuned in to how they are feeling.

Adaptability

Adaptable youngsters who're notably adaptable could be capable of transitioning from one hobby to some other without an awful lot of trouble. They may move from playtime to lunchtime to naptime, without having any problem.

Slow to conform: kids who're sluggish to adapt could have a tougher time shifting from one activity to another. They may react very strongly to being advised that playtime is over and might have a difficult time with one-of-a-kind transitions all through the day. Adaptable kids can also seem like greater "smooth," and you could no longer have a problem getting them to transport from one interest to some other throughout the day. Youngsters who're slower to adapt may additionally want more information and warnings from you while matters are going to alternate. Start giving warnings when your child will want to shift from one pastime to any other, like picking up their toys and heading into tub time. Slower to conform kids do higher when they understand what to expect, so attempt to preserve a regular ordinary.

Method/withdrawal

Drawing near: coming near children are excited and inclined to discover new things, people, and conditions. They may run to investigate a brand-new playground without hesitation and frequently will take little or no time to modify to new conditions.

Withdrawing: Chickening out kids is also referred to as "slow to warm up." They want extra time to adjust to new conditions and may hold again before they discover or be part of it. They will hesitate at a new social state of affairs rather than becoming a member of in proper away.

Patience

Excessive staying power: kids who are chronic will work hard to figure out precisely how that puzzle piece fits in, even though it is challenging. They will work very hard to finish something they've started and are possibly to practice something they need to grasp, like riding a motorcycle.

Low persistence: youngsters with low patience are more likely to move on to something else when they locate something tough. it is common place for them to be beaten when they conflict with something that is challenging for them. They may come to be very frustrated or ask for a person to do it for them. Children with excessive patience can be able to independently work via troubles without a great deal of adult assistance and may be more willing to work on duties by themselves. Mother and father may additionally want to check in with continual youngsters to see how they're doing while they're operating through trouble and provide assistance if the kid wishes it. Kids with low patience may additionally surrender fast or be overwhelmed with frustration after they discover a challenge hard. Help youngsters learn to get-up-and-go through the moods that go along with feeling beaten. coaching them strain control techniques like taking deep breaths or taking walks away for a few minutes can assist and encourage them to work through troubles on hard tasks.

Distractibility

High distractibility: fairly distractible kids will quickly shift their attention from one element to every other. They will not be capable of attention to a verbal exchange over dinner if they see a dog outside the kitchen window. They may be much attuned to information and have a hard time focusing in locations and areas which might be busy and loud.

Low distractibility: children with low distractibility find it easy to get centered on a challenge. They get absorbed in an e-book even though there's a noisy gathering of people in the equal room. These kids can block out many distractions and absolutely focus their attention on what they may be working on. Children who are without problems with distractibility might also want adult help to absolutely focus on a venture. Turn off the TV at some stage in homework time and discover quiet, calm places so youngsters can be attentive of what they need to be doing. Don't forget, distractible youngsters aren't being rude when they shift their interest; they are simply extra attuned to noticing matters of their surroundings. Kids who are not without problems of being distracted can be capable of being hyper-centered on the task at hand, however, many additionally find it difficult to move on while they're disenchanted with something; they'll generally tend to focus on the one negative emotion. Adults can help these children with the aid of giving them tools to use to control their emotions.

Mood

More superb temper: kids with a greater naturally high-quality temper is probable to seem glad and bubbly most of the time. They may have an easier time shifting on from durations of unhappiness. They tend to be greater construct and will regularly be cheery and upbeat in their interactions.

Extra poor temper: children who have an extra negative mood might also appear like greater subdued than glad. They will have a demeanor this is calmer and can seem gloomy, unhappy, or terrible. They will not display their emotions externally but experience bizarre matters.

it is regularly predicted of youngsters (and adults too) to be outwardly happy most of the time, however, there's nothing wrong with children (or adults) who have an extra poor mood. you can aid these kids via adjusting your expectancies—that your child might not appear outwardly satisfied all of the time. Understand that simply due to the fact they don't display it, doesn't suggest that they are now not

experiencing joy or happiness. Reassure your toddler

that their emotions and moods are valid and whatever

they feel is adequate. Be there to guide them and

teach them wholesome ways to express their

emotions.

HOW TEMPERAMENT AFFECTS US

Let us see briefly how temperament actually

influences our prayer lives. Temperament is the most

constitutional – or genetic – part of our character,

being mainly determined by biological factors.

Temperament cannot be changed but it can be shaped

into the likeness of Christ and controlled by the Holy

Spirit. It would be futile to expect a drastic change in

the genetic makeup of our person, but we can expect the 'polishing' work of the Holy Spirit. The new birth does not change temperament; although grace helps us to live with it. It emphasizes flexibility and a certain possibility of change. This is important because no one likes to be labeled in closed boxes. We should remember, too, that every human being is unique and therefore classifications are always somewhat relative. Stereotypes are the opposite of divine variety. Classification revolves around two fundamental axes:

- One's general attitude in life: introversion – extroversion:

- One's predominant psychological function. Described are four psychological types: thinking, feeling, sensorial and intuitive.

The prayer life of extroverts. Their natural tendency is towards action rather than meditation. They will be the ones doing things in the church because they like to be active all the time. Consequently, they find it difficult to maintain a regular prayer life. The more extrovert a person is, the more difficult they find it to pray and to concentrate while praying – too much to do! Introverts, on the other hand, are much more methodical and will set time apart. Extroverts find difficulty in cultivating their inner life, their thoughts and feelings flow spontaneously outwards. So beginning to pray is rather like having to make an enormous leap. They will usually choose praying with others rather than privately. Prayer meetings give them the opportunity to relate with others, which is precisely the source of energy they need to start praying. Once they are in the atmosphere of a group, they enjoy participation; this community flavor is just the kind of stimulus they need to warm them up spiritually. For them, prayer is linked with service and action. The focus of their requests is the needs of the world rather than the inner world, unlike the introvert.

THE THREE DIMENSIONS OF TEMPERAMENTS

Surgency/extraversion includes positive anticipation, impulsivity, increased levels of activity and a desire for sensation seeking. This factor reflects the degree to which a child is generally happy, active, and enjoys vocalizing and seeking stimulation, increased levels of smiling and laughter are observed in babies high in surgency/extraversion. 10 to 11-year-olds with higher levels of surgency/extraversion are more likely to develop externalizing problems like acting out; however, they are less likely to develop internalizing problems such as shyness and low self-esteem.

Negative effect

Negative effect includes fear, frustration, sadness, discomfort, and anger. This factor reflects the degree to which a child is shy and not easily calmed. Anger and frustration is seen as early as 2 to 3 months of age. Anger and frustration, together, predict externalizing and internalizing difficulties. Anger, alone, is later related to externalizing problems, while fear is associated with internalizing difficulties. Fear as evidenced by behavioral inhibition is seen as early as 7–10 months of age, and later predicts children's fearfulness and lower levels of aggression

Effortful control

Effortful control includes the focusing and shifting of attention, inhibitory control, perceptual sensitivity, and a low threshold for pleasure. This factor reflects the degree, to which a child can focus attention, is not easily distracted, can restrain a dominant response in order to execute a non-dominant response, and employ planning. When high in effortful control, 6 to 7-year-olds tend to be more empathetic and lower in aggressiveness. Higher levels of effortful control at age seven also predict

lower externalizing problems at age 11 years.

Children high on negative affect show decreased

internalizing and externalizing problems when they

are also high on effortful control.

CHAPTER 5

HOW TO DETERMINE ONE'S TEMPERAMENT

In order to determine one's temperament, it is not wise to study the bright or dark sides of each temperament and to apply them to oneself; one should first and foremost attempt to answer the three questions mentioned below.

1.   Do I react immediately and vehemently or slowly and superficially to a strong impression made upon me?

2.   Am I inclined to act at once or to remain calm and to wait?

3.   Does the excitement last for a long time or only for a short while?

Another very practical way to determine one's

temperament consists in considering one's reaction to

offenses, by asking these questions: Can I forgive

when offended? Do I bear grudges and resent insults?

If one must answer: usually I cannot forget insults, I

brood over them; to think of them excites me anew; I

can bear a grudge a long time, several days, nay,

weeks if somebody has offended me; I try to evade

those who have offended me, refuse to speak to them,

etc., then, one is either of choleric or melancholic

temperament. If on the contrary the answer is: I do

not harbor ill will; I cannot be angry with anybody

for a long time; I forget even actual insults very soon;

sometimes I decide to show anger, but I cannot do so,

at least not for a long time, at most an hour or two –

if such is the answer, then one is either sanguine or

phlegmatic. After having recognized that one is of the choleric or melancholic temperament the following questions should be answered: Am I quickly excited at offenses? Do I manifest my resentment by words or action? Do I feel inclined to oppose an insult immediately and retaliate? Or, do I at offenses received remain calm outwardly in spite of internal excitement? Am I frightened by offenses, disturbed, despondent, so that I do not find the right words or the courage for a reply, and therefore, remain silent? Does it happen repeatedly that I hardly feel the offense at the moment when I receive it, but a few hours later, or even the following day, feel it so much more keenly? In the first case, the person is choleric; in the second, melancholic. Upon ascertaining that one's temperament is either sanguine or phlegmatic one must inquire further: Am I suddenly inflamed with anger at offenses received; do I feel inclined to flare up and to act rashly? Or, do I remain quiet? Indifferent? Am I not easily swayed by my feelings? In the first case we are sanguine, in the second, phlegmatic. It is very important, and indeed necessary to determine, first of all, one's basic temperament by answering these questions, to be able to refer the various symptoms of the different temperaments to their proper source. Only then can self-knowledge be deepened to a full realization of how far the various light and dark sides of one's temperament are developed, and of the modifications and variations one's predominant temperament may have undergone by mixing with another temperament.

It is usually considered very difficult to recognize one's own temperament or that of another person. Experience, however, teaches that with proper guidance, even persons of moderate education can quite easily learn to know their own temperament, and that of associates and subordinates.

Greater difficulties, however, arise in discovering the temperament in the following instances:

1.   A person is habitually given to sin. In such cases the sinful passion influences man more than the temperament; for instance, a sanguine person, who by nature is very much inclined to live in peace and harmony with others can become very annoying and cause great trouble by giving way to envy and anger.

2.   A person has progressed very far on the path of

perfection. In such cases the dark sides of the temperament, as they manifest themselves, usually, in ordinary persons, can hardly be noticed at all. Saintly people of melancholic temperament never allow their naturally sad, morose, discouraging temperament to show itself.

3.   A person possesses only slight knowledge of himself. He neither recognizes his good or evil disposition, nor does he understand the intensity of his own evil inclinations and the degree of his excitability; consequently he will not have a clear idea of his temperament. If anyone tries to assist Him to know himself by questioning him, he gives false answers, not intentionally, but simply because he does not know himself. If such persons begin to

devote themselves to a more spiritual life, they can usually acquire a fairly reliable diagnosis of their temperament only after they have practiced meditation and examination of conscience for some length of time.

4.   A person is very nervous. With such persons the signs of nervousness, as restlessness, irritability, inconstancy of humor and resolution, the inclination to melancholy and discouragement, manifest themselves so forcibly that the symptoms of temperament are more or less obscured. It is especially difficult to discern the temperament of hysterical persons, if the so-called hysterical character is already fully developed.

5.   A person has a so-called mixed temperament.

Mixed temperaments are those in which one temperament predominates while another temperament also manifests itself. It will be a great help in such cases to know the temperaments of the parents of such person. If father and mother are of the same temperament, the children will probably inherit the temperament of the parents. If father and mother are of a choleric temperament, the children will also be choleric. If, however, the father and mother are of different temperaments, the children will inherit the different temperaments. If, for instance, the father is of a choleric temperament and the mother melancholic, the children will be either choleric with a melancholic mixture, or melancholic with a choleric tendency, according to the degree of influence of either of the two parents. In order to learn the predominant temperament, it is absolutely necessary to follow closely the above-mentioned questions concerning the temperaments. But it also happens, although not so often as many believe, that in one person two temperaments are so mixed that both are equally strong.

In this case it is naturally very hard to judge with which temperament the respective person is to be classified. It is probable, however, that in the course of time, e.g. on occasion of ordeals or difficulties one of the temperaments will manifest itself predominantly.

A very valuable help for the discernment of the mixed, and especially of the pure, temperaments is the expression of the eye and more or less the manner in which a person walks. The eye of the choleric is resolute, firm, energetic, fiery; the eye of the sanguine is cheerful, friendly, and careless; the eye of the melancholic looks more or less sad and troubled; the eye of the phlegmatic is faint, devoid of expression.

The choleric steps up firmly, resolutely, is more or less always in a hurry; the sanguine is light- footed and quick, his walking is often like dancing; the gait of the melancholic is slow and heavy; that of the phlegmatic is lazy and sluggish.

KNOWLEDGE a key Element

It may be difficult in many cases to decide upon the temperament of any particular person; still we should not permit ourselves to be discouraged in the attempt to understand our own temperament and that of those persons with whom we live or with whom we come often into contact, for the advantages of such insight are very great. To know the temperaments of our fellow men helps us to understand them better, treat them more correctly, bear with them more patiently. These are evidently advantages for social life which can hardly be appreciated enough.

A choleric person is won by quiet explanation of reasons and motives; whereas by harsh commands he is embittered, hardened, driven to strong-headed resistance.

A melancholic person is made suspicious and reticent by a rude word or an unfriendly mien; by continuous kind treatment, on the contrary, he is made pliable,

trusting, and affectionate.

A choleric person can be relied upon, but with a

sanguine person we can hardly count even upon his

apparently serious promises. Without a knowledge of

the temperaments of our fellow men we will treat

them often wrongly, to their and to our own

disadvantage. With a knowledge of the

temperaments, one bears with fellow men more

patiently. If one knows that their defects are the

consequence of their temperament, he excuses them

more readily and will not so easily be excited or

angered by them. He remains quiet, for instance,

even if a choleric is severe, sharp-edged, impetuous,

or obstinate. And if a melancholic person is slow,

hesitating, undecided; if he does not speak much and even if he says awkwardly the little he has to say; or if a sanguine person is very talkative, light-minded, and frivolous; if a phlegmatic cannot be aroused from his usual indifference, he does not become irritated. It is of the greatest benefit furthermore to recognize fully one's own temperament. Only if one knows it, can he judge correctly himself, his moods, his peculiarities, his past life. An elderly gentleman, of wide experience in the spiritual life, who happened to read the following treatise on temperaments said: "*I have never learned to know myself so well, as I find myself depicted in these lines, because nobody dared to tell me the truth as plainly as these lines have done.*"

If one knows one's own temperament, he can work

out his own perfection with greater assurance,

because finally the whole effort toward self-

perfection consists in the perfection of the good and

in the combating of the evil dispositions. Thus the

choleric will have to conquer, in the first place, his

obstinacy, his anger, his pride; the melancholic, his

lack of courage and his dread of suffering; the

sanguine, his talkativeness, his inconsistency; the

phlegmatic, his sloth, his lack of energy. The person

who knows himself will become more humble,

realizing that many good traits which he considered

to be virtues are merely good dispositions and the

natural result of his temperament, rather than

acquired virtues. Consequently the choleric will

judge more humbly of his strong will, his energy, and

his fearlessness; the sanguine of his cheerfulness, of his facility to get along well with difficult persons; the melancholic will judge more humbly about his sympathy for others, about his love for solitude and prayer; the phlegmatic about his good nature and his repose of mind. The temperament is innate in each person; therefore it cannot be exchanged for another temperament. But man can and must cultivate and perfect the good elements of his temperament and combat and eradicate the evil ones. Every temperament is in itself good and with each one man can do well and work out his salvation. It is, therefore, imprudent and ungrateful to wish to have another temperament. All of man's inclinations and peculiarities should be used for the service of the Lord and contribute to His honor and to man's welfare. Persons of various temperaments who live together should learn not to oppose but to support and supplement one another.

FINDING YOUR TEMPERAMENT

Why should one really be concerned about finding his temperament? If he cannot change it, why bother? The issue is not one of changing our temperament, but one of trying to understand better our actions and the actions of others about us. By knowing this, we should be in a better position to know how to deal with ourselves or others. The expressions: "Know thyself," "Examine you," "Accept thyself," have evidently come out of the felt need to know about ourselves. And by coming to know our temperament, we can concentrate on our strengths and strive to deal with our weaknesses much better and more effectively. While the temperament theory may not hold all the answers for a man's behavior; yet, it is one of the most helpful devices to explain much of the reasons for man's actions. If one can find which temperament or which blends of temperaments he is, then he should be able to better understand his actions and the actions of others. Temperament studies have become very helpful also in vocational guidance, testing for employment, and the avoidance of many problems in hiring the wrong person for a job. Special tests have been prepared to give help in evaluating people in certain situations. Some tests are simple while others are quite complicated, but all are designed to help suit a person to the best situation for his own happiness and the company's successful use

of his talents. Why can't the same principle be true in

the church as well? Through the finding of one's

temperament, the church is better able to make use of

his talents and abilities to help further the Lord's

Cause upon the earth.

CHAPTER 6

TEMPERAMENT AND EMOTION

The past lesson and this one are trying to show the need for man to deal with two eruptive emotions that cause most of the problems mankind faces: FEAR & ANGER. Both are well illustrated in Scripture (Holy book) as being detrimental to man's well-being. Of the two, anger is probably the one that causes more harm to mankind, especially in regards to marriage and the family, as well as other interpersonal relationships. Fear and anger can lead to a marriage that no longer has communication in it. The problem is not lack of communication, but anger or fear is the real culprits

THE MANY FORMS OF ANGER

Anger and its varied forms are acts and attitudes or conditions of the heart that are condemned by God as sinful, and therefore harmful to man. In order to continue in fellowship with God, the Christian must deal with this culprit (1 John 1:7). Those who will not deal with their anger cannot live peaceably with all men. A study of anger has led many to identify the following sixteen different attitudes and actions as related directly to anger:

Bitterness	*Malice*	*Clamor*	*Envy*	*Resentment*	*Intolerance*
Criticism	*Revenge*	*Wrath*	*Hatred*	*Sedition*	*Jealousy*
Attack	*Gossip*	*Sarcasm*	*Unforgiveness*		

It has already been suggested that temperaments are all predisposed to either fear or anger; and in some cases, a combination of two temperaments (Sanguine and

Melancholy) may predispose one to both fear and anger. But generally the two temperaments (Sanguine and Choleric) are predisposed more towards anger than fear. The only temperament that will not have an inherent problem with anger is the Phlegmatic. But since no one generally is 100% Phlegmatic, even this temperament may combine with another to have a tendency towards anger. Sanguine are instantly eruptive, but forgiving; while Choleric are eruptive, but grudging. Melancholies take longer to explode, but they are also capable of one or more forms of anger. The basic fundamental then of the relationship between temperament and anger or fear is in their reserve(introvert) or their extrovert nature. ***The more introverted the more problem with fear. The more extroverted, the more problem with anger.***

TEMPERAMENT AND STRESS

Stress or pressure is a part of most, if not all, of our lives. It can be good for us, but at the same time, depending on how it is handled, it can be bad and bring on undesirable conditions. The good part about stress is that it keeps things moving, going, active. Without pressure or stress much less would be accomplished by all of us. So, it plays a very good role in all of our lives. But when not handled as it should be, the following illustration to the right can show the outcome:

There are many things that help to bring stress or pressure in our lives, but some of these can be more challenging to deal with than others. The following list will illustrate:

1. Trying to satisfy all and desiring to avoid conflict.

2. In constant contact with the poor, sick, dying, nursing homes, etc.

3. Role confusion.

4. Not able to protect one's personal boundaries for rest and recreation with family.

5. Not properly dealing with guilt in one's life.

6. Uncertainty of job, or health, or one's marriage, etc.

7. Loneliness.

8. Death of close family member.

When stress continues over a long period of time without being properly dealt with, it can bring all kinds of diseases, such as: Hyper-tension, Stroke, Heart Diseases, Ulcers, Tension, Arthritis, etc. Nothing is more important than our health, however, it can affect our spiritual life as well. It can cause a person to forsake the Lord, turn their back on active service in His kingdom, and become so self-centered that they do not reach out to others. So stress or pressure must be dealt with properly to avoid the bad effect in our lives. But what does all of this have to do with Temperaments? Since all human beings will face some stressful situations in their lives, how does each temperament handle such? It should be interesting to see how each reacts to stress.

CONCLUSION

SANGUINE TEMPERAMENT

1.   Is self-composed, seldom shows signs of embarrassment, perhaps forward or bold.

2.   Eager to express himself before a group; likes to be heard.

3.   Prefers group activities; work or play; not easily satisfied with individual projects.

4.   Not insistent upon acceptance of his ideas or plans; agrees readily with others' wishes; compliant and yielding.

5.   Good in details; prefers activities requiring pep and energy.

6.   Impetuous and impulsive; his decisions are often (usually) wrong.

7.   Keenly alive to environment, physical and social; likes curiosity.

8.   Tends to take success for granted. Is a follower; lacks initiative.

9.   Hearty and cordial, even to strangers; forms acquaintanceship easily.

10.   Tends to elation of spirit; not given to worry and anxiety; is carefree.

11.   Seeks wide and broad range of friendships; is not selective; not exclusive in games.

12.   Quick and decisive in movements; pronounced or excessive energy output.

13.   Turns from one activity to another in rapid succession; little perseverance.

14.   Makes adjustments easily; welcomes changes; makes the best appearance possible.

15.   Frank, talkable, sociable, emotions readily expressed; does not stand on ceremony.

16.   Frequent fluctuations of mood; tends to frequent alterations of elation and depression.

CHOLERIC TEMPERAMENT

1.   Is self-composed; seldom shows embarrassment, is forward or bold.

2.   Eager to express himself before a group if he has some purpose in view.

3.   Insistent upon the acceptance of his ideas or plans; argumentative and persuasive.

4.   Impetuous and impulsive; plunges into situations whore forethought would have deterred him.

5.   Self-confident and self-reliant; tends to take success for granted.

6.   Strong initiative; tends to elation of spirit; seldom gloomy or moody; prefers to lead.

7.   Very sensitive and easily hurt; reacts strongly to praise or blame.

8.   Not given to worry or anxiety.

9.   Quick and decisive in movement; pronounced or excessive energy output.

10.   Marked tendency to persevere; docs not abandon something readily regardless of success.

11.   Emotions not freely or spontaneously expressed, except anger.

12.   Makes best appearance possible; perhaps conceited; may use hypocrisy, deceit, disguise.

MELANCHOLIC TEMPERAMENT

1.   Is self-conscious, easily embarrassed, timid, and bashful.

2.   Avoids talking before a group; when obliged to he finds it difficult. Prefers to work and play alone. Good in details; careful.

3. Deliberative; slow in making decisions; perhaps overcautious even in minor matters.

4. Lacking in self-confidence and initiative; compliant and yielding.

5. Tends to detachment from environment; reserved and distant except to intimate friends.

6. Tends to depression; frequently moody or gloomy; very sensitive; easily hurt.

7. Does not form acquaintances readily; prefers narrow range of friends; tends to exclude others.

8. Worries over possible misfortune; crosses bridges before coming to them.

9. Secretive; seclusive; shut in; not inclined to speak unless spoken to.

10. Slow in movement; deliberative or perhaps indecisive; moods frequent and constant.

11, Often represents himself at a disadvantage; modest and unassuming.

PHLEGMATIC TEMPERAMENT

1.   Deliberative; slow in making decisions; perhaps overcautious in minor matters. Indifferent to external affairs.

2.   Reserve and distant.

3.   Slow in movement.

4.   Marked tendency to persevere.

www.ingramcontent.com/pod-product-compliance
Lightning Source LLC
Chambersburg PA
CBHW070528160726
48003CB00004B/1731